A Nest
of Aliens

DAVID ORME

A Nest of Aliens
by David Orme
Illustrated by Jorge Mongiovi and Ulises Carpintero
Cover photograph: © blackred

Published by Ransom Publishing Ltd.
Radley House, 8 St. Cross Road, Winchester, Hampshire, SO23 9HX, UK
www.ransom.co.uk

ISBN   978 184167 467 4

First published in 2011
Reprinted 2013, 2014

Originally published in 1998 by Stanley Thornes Publishers Ltd.

A CIP catalogue record of this book is available from the British Library.

CONTENTS

NOT FOR THE PUBLIC TO KNOW

TOP SECRET
ZONE 13 FILES ONLY

4

MISSING ON THE MOUNTAIN

Nick Owen thought he had the best job in the world. He worked in the mountains of North Wales.

He was a National Park warden. If people got into trouble on the mountains, Nick would be there to help them. He did his best to make sure people didn't do anything too stupid.

Every year, though, three or four people died in the mountains. The mist could come down quickly and trap people. Sometimes people set out without the right equipment or clothing, even when the weather was bad.

Today, Nick was feeling worried. Over the last month, four people had disappeared on the mountain where he patrolled. What was very surprising was that no bodies had been found.

He couldn't understand it. People can't just disappear!

He looked in his diary. On June the first, two people, a man and a woman, hadn't come back from walking on the mountain. Four days later, two more people went missing.

That had been last week. Since then, search parties had gone all over the mountain. No trace of them had been found.

000//000

Nick parked his 4 x 4 outside the headquarters of the National Park. There was a meeting today about the missing people.

Jim Evans was in charge of the wardens. Nick usually talked to him in the Welsh language. There were people at the meeting who spoke only English, so today Nick spoke in that language.

The people from the mountain rescue team were ready to give up.

'I don't think they're missing at all,' said Roger, their leader. 'I think they've gone home without telling anyone.'

'But what about their tents?' said Nick. 'They wouldn't leave those behind!'

'I agree with Roger,' said Jim. 'I went all over the mountain yesterday. The weather wasn't bad last week. I think they've gone home.'

That afternoon, Nick set off for the mountain. He had an idea. It was dangerous, but it was worth a try.

NOT FOR THE PUBLIC TO KNOW
TOP SECRET
ZONE 13 FILES ONLY

THE HIDDEN VALLEY

The mountain was quite safe, if people were careful. But there was one very dangerous place.

On one side of the mountain, there was a hidden valley. In this valley, many years ago, slate had been mined. These days, people didn't use so much slate for their roofs. The mine had been closed down fifty years ago. In the walls of the valley there were tunnels that ran into the heart of the mountain. The tunnels

were very dangerous. The roof could easily cave in, leaving people trapped. Maybe the missing people had stupidly wandered into the tunnels.

Nick was cross with himself. He should have thought of it before.

ooo//ooo

It was a long climb to the hidden valley. It was in a quiet part of the mountain. Very few people went there. Usually the ground was wet and boggy, and walking was difficult. This spring it had been dry.

A little sheep path ran down into the valley. Nick sat on a flat rock at the top of the valley for a rest.

He looked down. There was the valley, peaceful as usual. Wait a minute! What was that?

Something strange was happening in the valley. Right in the centre was a flat place. There were ruins of old mine buildings there. The air seemed to be shaking. It was like the shimmer you sometimes see over a hot road.

The shimmering was changing. A grey shadow seemed to be creeping over the valley. It became more and more solid. Nick gasped. This couldn't be true!

Even though it was there in front of his eyes, he couldn't believe it.

It was huge, and round, and made of grey metal. Nick had seen nothing like it.

Nothing on Earth.

IN THE MINE

Nick had read about UFOs, or Unidentified Flying Objects, but he didn't believe in aliens from space. That was just rubbish! But this looked just like the pictures he had seen.

He quickly took his camera out of his backpack. He took lots of photographs. If it was a flying saucer, the pictures would be worth a fortune!

Just then, the great grey object disappeared! It was as if it had never been there.

Nick blinked. The valley looked peaceful again. He couldn't have imagined it!

He set off down the narrow sheep path to the bottom of the valley. When he got there, he started walking across the place where the UFO had been.

Suddenly, he walked into something invisible. Luckily he had been walking slowly, or he would have bruised himself badly. He felt with his hands. It was smooth, and felt like metal.

He walked all round the strange, invisible object. On the other side of it was a steep valley wall. This was the place where the old mine tunnels were.

He peered into one of the tunnels. It was dark and cold. He could hear water running inside.

Then Nick saw something lying on the ground. He walked a little way into the tunnel.

It was a walker's map! Someone had been here! Could the missing people be in the old mine workings?

Nick knew it wasn't safe to go into the tunnel alone. He would go back and get help.

He turned to walk out of the tunnel.

In the entrance to the tunnel were two figures. They were just shadows against the bright sunlight. Even so, Nick knew two things. They were carrying weapons – and they weren't human.

The two figures walked into the tunnel. It was still difficult to see them clearly. They had big heads, but Nick couldn't really see their faces. Their arms and legs seemed very long and thin.

Then, to Nick's amazement, they spoke – in English!

PRISONERS!

'Walk down the tunnel,' said one of the aliens, in a strange, squeaky voice. 'We have weapons.'

Nick could see that. The weapons were stubby and black. Nick wondered how they worked. Did they fire bullets? Or was it something worse?

He soon found out. He didn't move fast enough for the aliens. One of them fired at his leg. He suddenly felt a terrible pain – it was as if his leg was on fire!

Nick yelled out in agony. Then, suddenly, the pain was gone! He looked down at his leg. There was no injury at all!

'Now, move,' said the alien.

Nick moved.

The tunnel turned a corner. It didn't look much like an old mine now. The walls were smooth, like cement. A light was coming from somewhere. It seemed to glow from the walls.

Nick turned to get a better look at the aliens, but they waved their weapons at him and he turned away quickly. He didn't want to face that terrible pain again!

The aliens stopped.

'Wait,' one of them said.

Part of the wall at the side of the tunnel started to change. It looked like a grey mist. Then it disappeared. A doorway!

The aliens pointed their weapons. Nick walked though the doorway. Immediately, the wall behind him went solid again.

Nick was in a small room. On the floor were three people: two women and a skinny, feeble-looking man. They were three of the missing walkers!

The three of them had been given a hard time. The aliens had given them water, but no food. They were starving.

There had been four of them to start with. The aliens had taken one of them away, and he had not come back. One of the women was very upset. The missing man was her boyfriend.

'We were all taken to a big cave,' said one of the women. 'They did things to us. I think they were tests. It was terrible. We were tied down and they cut off bits of our skin.'

'We were pushed back into here,' said the other woman. 'But Simon didn't come back with us.'

'Yesterday, someone else was pushed in here,' said the man. 'A tall guy, with dark hair. He was about to tell us who he was when they took him away.'

Just then the wall behind Nick went misty. The aliens were back!

They pointed their weapons at Nick.

'Come.'

He set off down the tunnel again. The aliens walked behind him. Nick guessed he was going to be tested.

It didn't sound as if he was going to enjoy it.

THE UNDERGROUND LABORATORY

The tunnel opened out into a huge cave. One end of it had been set up as a laboratory. There were strange machines along the walls. In the centre of the cave was a tall, clear tube. With a shock, Nick realised that there was a man inside it! What terrible experiment was going on here?

Nearby was a flat table. Straps hung at the sides. Nick guessed that he was going to end up on that table.

He glanced in despair towards the far end of the cave. In a flash, he realised that he had been here before!

Only one end of the cave had been turned into the alien laboratory. The rest of the cave was just as the old slate miners had left it. Two years ago, Nick had helped to rescue some cave explorers who had got lost in the underground passage. In the corner of the cave there had been a shaft leading to lower levels. If only he could get there!

At that moment the man in the glass tube moved. He started to scream. It was a scream of fear, not of pain. For an instant, the guards were distracted.

Nick dashed towards the dark corner of the cave. There were shouts behind him. Nick felt a terrible pain as the weapons were fired at him. But he had reached the shaft!

There had been an old wooden ladder in the shaft. It was still there! Nick scrambled over the edge and started down.

After a few metres he found his feet were dangling in mid-air. The rest of the ladder was missing!

The aliens had reached the top of the shaft by now. They fired down at him. His hands caught the full blast. With a scream Nick let go. He was falling ...

6

THE SHAFT

Seconds later, he hit freezing water. He sank down, down.

At last he managed to push his way to the surface. He had fallen right past the tunnel that would take him out of the mine. He had fallen to the flooded levels at its deepest part.

It was pitch dark. Nick managed to swim to the wall of the shaft. He put his hands up – and found a ledge!

Nick pulled himself out of the water. He felt
a tunnel all round him.

Of course, this was one of the old tunnels
that drained water out of the mine. Spring
had been dry and the water levels had
dropped. If he followed the tunnel, he might
get out!

ooo//ooo

It took him hours to walk along the tunnel
in the complete darkness. Many times he
bruised his head and body as he bumped into
the walls. Once he fell. When he got up again
he was worried in case he had turned round

in the dark and was heading back towards the water-filled shaft.

At last he saw a faint light ahead. Minutes later, he was blinking in the evening sunshine.

He still had his backpack, but he needed to move quickly to get help. He hid it carefully under a bush near the tunnel entrance. He would come back for it later.

Nick set off down the mountain.

ooo//ooo

He reached the National Park headquarters at last. The walk had dried Nick's clothes. A light was on in Jim's office. Nick knocked and went in.

'Jim!' he said. 'You're not going to believe this ...'

Jim was sitting behind his desk.

He was holding one of the alien weapons in his hand, and he was pointing it at Nick.

BACK AT H.Q.

'Sit down, Nick.'

Nick sat. He couldn't believe what was happening.

'Jim! What's going on? You're not an alien!'

'Oh yes I am.'

'What do you mean?'

'I mean that I'm only Jim on the outside. The real Jim is dead. We select the bodies we want, and move in. I think those prisoners told you someone else had been captured. That was Jim.'

'Why are you doing this?'

'Our planet is too old. It is dying. This planet is young, but the gravity is too strong for us to be comfortable. So we need your bodies.

'Our base in the mountain is only the first. Our experiments have been successful. Soon millions of my people will be arriving. Now you know this, you will come back to the mountain with me. You are strong. Your body will suit us well.'

Nick knew that wasn't going to happen. He would rather die. With a yell, he leapt at Jim's throat.

Jim fired. Nick's body turned to a grey mist. The air shimmered. He was gone.

ooo//ooo

'What a pity,' thought the alien that looked like Jim. 'Never mind, this world is full of good, strong bodies. We'll move in, slowly. No one will ever find out – until it is too late!'

ooo//ooo

Two days later, someone found Nick's backpack.

'A camera!' he thought. 'I wonder what pictures are on it?'

He turned on the camera and looked at the screen.

NOT FOR THE PUBLIC TO KNOW

TOP SECRET

ZONE 13 FILES ONLY

ABOUT THE AUTHOR

David Orme is an expert on strange, unexplained events. For his protection (and yours) we cannot show a photograph of him.

David created the Zone 13 files to record the cases he studied. Some of these files really do involve aliens, but many do not. Aliens are not everywhere. Just in most places.

These stories are all taken from the Zone 13 files. They will not be here for long. Read them while you can.

But don't close your eyes when you go to sleep at night. **They** will be watching you.